AF605366

FENCES
OF AUSTRALIA

FENCES OF AUSTRALIA

JACK BRADSHAW

CONTENTS

PREFACE

Previous page: Jarrah split post and wire fence near Manjimup, WA, is typical of early fencing throughout the south-west.

Opposite: Gates at Coonatto Station, 70 km east of Port Augusta, SA. The station once covered 2300 sq km, where 130,000 sheep were shorn.

Page 9: One of the more bizarre fence materials used around a WA wheatbelt homestead.

Fences in the rural landscape are prosaic affairs. They denote ownership and they contain or exclude various kinds of stock. But they are more than that. A well-built post and rail or stone fence, for example, is a thing of beauty, a monument to pride in workmanship and a cause for wonder at the skill and hard work involved. A well-ordered farm with fences to demarcate the paddocks may signify enterprise and success, while an old decaying fence, half covered by sand, invokes an image of a failed venture, hardship and despair. Rural fences are uncompromisingly practical; they exist only to serve a purpose. A good fencer, however, takes pride in producing a 'workman-like' job because, while they may not be built for show, fences will be there for all to see for many years.

The materials, design and method of construction reveal a great deal about the surrounding landscape, the type of farming enterprise and even the economic conditions of the time. This is especially so for older fences, which were always made with the materials most readily available. Tracing the history of fencing in Australia reveals many of the fascinating changes in social and economic conditions that stimulated fencing inventions and developments.

Apart from this fascination, there were two things that piqued my interest in fences. The first occurred when I was about six years old and lived in the small mill town of Mornington in Western Australia. My school teacher, who also boarded with us, was transferred to a school at Gate 69 on the Rabbit Proof Fence at the end of her first year. No one had the faintest clue where Gate 69 might be and I have no idea how she finally got there. Years later I located the site of the Gate 69 school, now long gone. It turned out to be 69 miles south of Cunderdin on the 1165 kilometre long No. 2 Rabbit Proof Fence. The school operated for five years from 1942 to 1947 and served just six families.

The second insight came when I was visiting the Yale University forest in Connecticut. This was forest that had regrown on cleared farmland after it had been abandoned for the more productive agricultural land in the Midwest of the United States in the mid-1800s. Stone fences from the original farms remained throughout the forest. My guide pointed out that it was possible to determine whether the adjacent paddocks were used for grazing or hay-making by the size of the stones used for packing between the two 'skins' of the fence, hay paddocks being picked clean of even the smallest stones.

Seeking out fences to photograph has given me an excuse to travel to all parts of Australia. These symbolic structures give cause to think about the lives of the people who built them and wonder at their skills and enterprise.

THE FIRST FENCES

Opposite and overleaf: The fish traps in Oyster Harbour, WA, were built by the Menang Noongar people 7000 years ago and are still evident today.

The first fences in Australia were built by Aboriginal people. The first to be recorded were those in Oyster Harbour near Albany, Western Australia, by the navigator Captain George Vancouver in 1791. These were in the form of fish traps used to contain fish in estuaries and rivers so they could then be caught at leisure. Numerous traps were observed in the harbour and in the Kalgan River. Some were made of sticks stuck into the sand at close intervals, while others were made of stone or a combination of both. Fish either entered the trap at high tide and became trapped as the tide ebbed or were herded into it before the trap was closed. The fish were then speared or caught by hand and thrown ashore.

Similar fish traps were later found all around Australia. The Brewarrina fish trap on the Barwon River in New South Wales was made of stones and designed to trap fish regardless of whether the river level was high or low. It was one of the largest of its kind with separate sections being used and maintained by different family groups. Due to the productivity of this fish trap it was the centre of large gatherings for trade and ceremonial purposes.

One of the most sophisticated systems was found at Lake Condah, about 20 kilometres inland from the south coast of Victoria, where an elaborate system of fences and ditches was used to trap fish and eels as far back as 8000 years ago. It is believed that eels may even have been held in these traps to be fattened up before they were harvested – perhaps Australia's first aquaculture venture.

SHEPHERDING TO FENCING

A palisade fence of the type commonly built in early colonial times to keep stock out of gardens and crops. This one, built 150 years later, was used to contain sheep ready for shearing.

Until the 1840s there were relatively few fences in Australia. The first fences to be erected by the members of the First Fleet in 1788 were paling or palisade fences – split palings or small posts buried in trenches in the ground. They were mainly designed to protect crops and gardens from wandering stock animals, rather than to contain the stock that initially were shepherded by day and yarded at night. It was ten years before the first post and rail fences were constructed to fence larger farms, either to contain or exclude stock.

The problem of herding rather than fencing in cattle was demonstrated very early in the New South Wales colony. A herd of black Cape cattle (four cows and two bulls) imported with the First Fleet were pastured on the Domain in Sydney under the eye of a convict cowherd and yarded at night in what is now the Royal Botanic Garden. Six months later all but one of the cows had escaped into the bush and were not found for another seven years – 50 kilometres away at the 'Cowpastures' – by which time they had grown to sixty head and were completely wild.

For the management of sheep, shepherding was the norm for the first sixty years of colonial history. Shepherds were white, Aboriginal or from the Pacific Islands and, especially in earlier times, were often convicts or ticket-of-leave men. Most were men but female shepherds were not uncommon. Their job was to move the sheep to pasture and water, prevent them from straying and generally attend to their wellbeing. Flocks were yarded at night as a protection against dingoes and, in some areas, losses to Aboriginal people who, naturally enough, regarded sheep roaming on their lands as fair game. The usual arrangement was that one or two shepherds, each with their own flock, would come back to an outstation at night where there was a hut and a set of portable folds made with hurdles or a more permanent yard made of brush. A hut keeper at the outstation served as the cook and the nightwatchman. The hut keeper lived separately in a 'shepherd's box' (a 2 metre x 1 metre portable box on legs which was shifted with the fold). With the aid of a dog and a fire he protected the sheep from dingoes during the night. Until the 1840s flock sizes for each shepherd were in the order of five hundred sheep.

For the management of sheep, shepherding was the norm for the first sixty years of colonial history.

Where dingoes were not a problem, especially after the availability of strychnine in the 1840s, open camping (which avoided the necessity of nightly yarding) became more common. Open camping had the advantage that the sheep spent more time eating than travelling – this meant they put on more weight and wool and were less likely to suffer footrot caused by conditions in the yards. Open camping also made it possible to increase each shepherd's flock to as many as three thousand sheep, and it remained that way until shepherding came to an end in the 1870s. The exception was in the north of Australia where shepherding continued into the 1930s. This change was partly influenced by the higher cost of wages that resulted when free convict labour was no longer available. Shepherding remained particularly important in Western Australia, where shepherds were required to keep stock away from the poison plant *Gastrolobium* until it could be fenced out or eradicated from paddocks.

Life for most shepherds was lonely and hard. In earlier times, many were working at the frontier of white settlement and frequently came into conflict with Aboriginal people, often caused by issues of their own making. The shepherds' wages and conditions were poor and often made worse when sheep losses were deducted from their wages. On some stations, incentives were paid for high lambing rates or shepherds would be allowed to keep one third, or some other agreed rate, of the lambs. Aboriginal shepherds were supplied with the same rations but were paid about half or even less the rate of white shepherds – although it was understood that some sheep would be killed to supply their relatives.

In closely settled areas most cattle were contained by fencing, while in more remote areas cattle were allowed to graze freely with little or no shepherding and were only mustered when required, not unlike modern-day practices.

Most of the grazing was carried out by squatters, who either occupied the land illegally or later through an annual licence. They had no security of tenure, nor did they receive any compensation for improvements should they be evicted. They had no incentive to invest in expensive fencing. Despite the fact that the productive advantages of fencing had been advocated for centuries, it took the coming together of several events in the 1840s and 1850s before large-scale fencing became viable in Australia.

The first of these was the availability of strychnine for poisoning dingoes. Without dingoes there was no need for nightly yarding and therefore open camping could be used. In Tasmania, where there were no dingoes, open camping was common and fencing was adopted much earlier as it required no protective shepherding.

At about the same time, legislative changes were made that provided settlers more secure land tenure under long-term lease or freehold. The huge increase in population as a result of the gold rushes in Victoria also created pressure for land to be made available for selection by farmers. To protect their position many squatters bought the freehold and needed to fence it to establish ownership and to facilitate open camping without the need for shepherds. Most freehold was granted under conditional purchase and prospective landowners were required to invest in a certain level of improvements before the grant was issued. Fencing contributed towards improvements.

The final event that changed the nature of flock control was the availability of iron and, later, steel wire. But wire was not a cheap fencing option initially and for many years

To protect their position many squatters bought the freehold and needed to fence it to establish ownership and to facilitate open camping without the need for shepherds.

it was comparable in cost to post and rail or stone fences, both of which continued to be built into the 1890s. Wire fences did have the advantage that they could be used where suitable timber or stone was not available. The use of fencing increased exponentially from the 1860s and by 1910, 2.2 million kilometres of (mostly post and wire) fences had been built in eastern Australia and shepherding had virtually ended.

> The final event that changed the nature of flock control was the availability of iron and, later, steel wire. But wire was not a cheap fencing option initially and for many years it was comparable in cost to post and rail or stone fences, both of which continued to be built into the 1890s.

Fencing provided a number of benefits for farm management: stock could be separated, allowing for better control of breeding – one of the factors in the reported increase in production; stocking rates could be increased, although the downside was that this was not always sustainable; lambing percentage was increased; diseases such as footrot were reduced; and there were considerable savings in wages. One report from 1867 claimed a 36 per cent cost saving, including the interest cost on the investment in fencing. Graziers increasing their stock production were able to take advantage of the huge rise in demand for meat as a consequence of the 1850s gold rush.

In the early stages the benefits were not universal. In some cases the replacement of the shepherd with the boundary rider, more interested in fence maintenance than sheep, led to the neglect of the flocks and poorer pasture management, especially on larger runs.

DITCHES, BRUSH, PALINGS AND PALISADES

This ninety-year-old hybrid split rail/paling fence surrounded an orchard at Deeside near Manjimup, WA. The palings were used to exclude pigs and rabbits.

The first fences to be built in Australia by Europeans were paling fences, made simply with vertical pieces of split wood, either spaced or butted together with the bottom end buried in a trench. The early paling fences were unsupported but the later addition of a rail at the top improved their stability. Sometimes the uprights were bound together with wire. A variation of this form of fencing is the palisade fence, made of small round posts. Until recent times the palisade fence was being used for sheep yards in more remote areas, where durable species of timber such as mulga (*Acacia aneura*), jam (*Ac. acuminata*) and cypress (*Callitris* sp.) were readily available.

A further development of the paling fence was the addition of posts and a bottom rail. This avoided the need to bury the ends – a valuable feature when non-durable wood was used. These solid structures were strong enough to contain pigs and sheep, and they were also used to keep out rabbits. Although they were simple to construct and could be made with logs from small trees or palings split from larger trees, the disadvantage was the large amount of material required. For that reason their use was generally restricted to yard building, although some extensive palisade fences were built where dense stands of jam or other small trees occurred. Some relatively large orchard paddocks were fenced with paling fences to keep out rabbits or pigs.

Farmers in Queensland and New South Wales used paling fences to keep out dingoes in the 1850s and part of the boundary between the two states was defined by a paling fence in the 1900s.

The first known brush fences appeared in the 1820s. These simple structures were made by piling up the trunks and branches of the small trees and shrubs that were cleared from the land. They were easier to build with unskilled labour, the materials were usually immediately at hand and they were reasonably stock proof – and they were by far the cheapest to build, an important consideration for struggling farmers or those squatters with no security of tenure. The main drawback was that they were very vulnerable to fire.

The first known brush fences appeared in the 1820s. These simple structures were made by piling up the trunks and branches of the small trees and shrubs that were cleared from the land.

Three variations on the brush or log fence.

Above: A light brush fence made from scrub readily to hand to control sheep in the Murchison, WA. A palisade fence is in the background.

Above, right: Larger logs were dragged to the fence line to make more permanent sheep yards on Dunlop Station on the Darling River in the 1880s.

Right: Three large karri logs were all that was needed to form a horse yard at the stables in a bush camp in the karri forest in the 1920s. PHOTO COURTESY OF UNDERWOOD COLLECTION

Above, left: Rail and palisade sheep yards at the shearing shed on the old Koonalda Station, SA, now part of the Nullarbor National Park.

Above: Rail and palisade cattle yards on the Gunbarrel Highway, WA. PHOTO COURTESY OF RICHARD SHUARD

Left: A rail and paling fence at Jondaryan woolshed near Oakey, Queensland.

During the rabbit plague of the late 1800s another disadvantage emerged: they were havens for rabbits. So much so that the Rabbit Inspector (at least in South Australia) had authority to burn the fences.

Nevertheless, these brush fences served their purpose and in some places were still being built two hundred years later, especially for outback sheep yards.

A variation of brush fencing is the log fence, made in the same way but requiring horse or bullock power to drag larger material into the fence. An extreme example of this could be found in some logging camps in the karri forest of Western Australia in the 1930s, where three karri logs were all that was required to create a horse-proof stable yard.

A more sophisticated version of the brush fence was the 'drop brush fence'. This consisted of two posts, about 30 centimetres apart, spaced to suit the length of the available brush. The brush was dropped between the posts which were then tied at the top with green hide or wire.

Although in Britain ditches had been used for centuries to control cattle and pigs and sometimes deer, they were not common in Australia. But ditches were used in the early days of the Swan River Colony to demarcate the boundaries of the various land grants along the Swan River. At half a metre deep they would have taken considerable effort to construct and it is not clear why they were built in preference to other forms of fencing. Post and rail, brush and wattle fences existed on the same properties at the same time. They did, however, indicate ownership and satisfied some of the requirement for 'improvements' that were necessary to retain the land grant. Evidence of ditches was still visible near Guildford, in the north of Perth, 170 years later.

BRUCE ROCK 77

POST AND RAIL

This reconstructed fence at the old bakery, Greenhills, WA, is a variation of the Harper fence, constructed of separate panels rather than overlapping rails.

In the closely settled areas of Australia, which were mostly well forested in the early days, the post and rail fence became the standard for fencing, for small holdings at least, from 1798. It quickly became a symbolic image of rural Australia, eventually enclosing thousands of hectares of land.

The simplest post and rail fence consisted of pairs of closely spaced posts (about the same diameter as the rails), each pair spaced according to the length of the rails. The rails were dropped between the posts, alternating between panels. The posts were then tied at the top with green hide or wire to stop them spreading. The advantage of this form of fence was that it could be built with unskilled labour using rails from small diameter trees or from saplings.

These fences were variously known as a 'double post and rail', a 'drop fence', a 'sapling fence' or, in Western Australia, a 'Harper fence'. The Harper fence, named after an early Beverley settler, was usually made with jam and was a popular form of fencing in the 1880s and 1890s in the farming areas of the Great Southern region. It was a much more efficient use of timber than the palisade fence that had commonly been built before. For many farmers a jam Harper fence was 'good for a generation or two' and was much preferred to the more expensive wire fence with an 'average twenty years' life'. A variation on the Harper fence used a double set of posts to contain the rails, the fence being made up of a series of independent panels.

In the closely settled areas of Australia, which were mostly well forested in the early days, the post and rail fence became the standard for fencing, for small holdings at least, from 1798. It quickly became a symbolic image of rural Australia, eventually enclosing thousands of hectares of land.

With a readily available resource of suitable trees, the more sophisticated split rail post and rail fence was economical to build but it required considerable skill. The first skill to learn, and possibly the most difficult, was selecting a good 'splitter'. A suitable tree had to be straight-grained and a reasonably durable species. Not all trees of a particular species are good 'splitters' and it required a good eye and experience to pick one. It made the difference between a comparatively easy job and an impossible one. In Western Australia, jarrah (*Eucalyptus marginata*) was the only species suitable, although a few fences were made with blackbutt (*Eucalyptus patens*). A variety of species of stringy bark and iron bark were used in eastern Australia.

Above: A jarrah split post and rail fence built in the 1970s in Manjimup, WA.

Above, right: A modern post and rail fence where both the posts and the rails are cut with a chainsaw, rather than being split. The mortise and tenons are also cut with a chainsaw. PHOTO COURTESY OF SUE BRADSHAW

Right: The durability of jam is demonstrated in this Harper fence, now more than 100 years old, at Mourambine, WA.

A three-rail jarrah split rail fence near Pemberton, WA (left), and a hybrid split rail/paling fence at Perup, WA (right).

Rails, generally between 2.1 and 2.4 metres long and 20–24 centimetres deep, are split using wedges, maul and axe. Where the trees are relatively small, the rails are split tangentially or 'on the back', producing a round-backed rail. Where larger trees are available, they are split radially or 'on the quarter' and require a log of at least 60 centimetres diameter. The ends of the rails are tapered with an axe (or more easily with an adze) to make a tenon about 15 centimetres deep. Mortises (about 5 x 18 centimetres) are cut into the posts using either a mortising axe or an auger and chisel. Using a mortising axe – essentially a felling axe cut down to a 50 millimetre face – requires great skill and would only be attempted by the best axemen.

The most challenging task in building a split rail fence is finding a tree that is a good 'splitter', even among the normally straight-grained jarrah.

The tenons for the rails are overlapped in the mortise and protrude to the other side. Tenons can be fitted tightly into the mortise (most common in Western Australia) or more loosely so that panels can be taken out without the need to remove a post. Two-rail fences were the most common but three rails (and even four or five rails) were also used where necessary, especially for stockyards.

Before the days of creosote, the buried ends of the split posts were often charred in a fire to make them more resistant to termites and rot. Fences, particularly the posts, made of less durable species might last only ten to twenty years but those made of durable species might last one hundred years with very little maintenance. Post and rail fences were not only built from local materials. In 1854 alone Tasmania exported sufficient sawn and split posts, rails and split palings to the mainland for more than 1000 kilometres of fencing.

Sawn post and rail fences are the favoured fence type for horse studs and training centres at Harvey, WA (left), Benger, WA (top), and Angaston, SA (bottom).

Fencing remained relatively rare on larger farms where stock were controlled mainly by shepherding until the 1850s, when wire started to become available. The building of post and rail fencing began to decline from that time, despite the cost being comparable for a number of years. On smaller farms, where timber and labour were more readily available than cash for wire, post and rail fences continued to be popular into the 1890s and even into the 1920s in some places. An unusual example of extensive split rail fencing is the impressive 3.5 kilometres of four-railed jarrah fence built around a 120 hectare horse paddock at Deeside in Western Australia in the early 1900s.

Recent years have seen a resurgence in popularity of post and rail fences, partly for aesthetics and partly for practical reasons. While a few are still made in the traditional manner, the modern post and rail is more commonly made with a chainsaw. In these fences the rails are cut tangentially from smaller diameter logs and the tenons and mortises are all cut with a chainsaw. The rails are usually set with the round side out. While not the same as a traditional fence to the purist, they are nevertheless an attractive and highly practical, solid, low maintenance fence and they too require considerable skill to make well.

The other form of post and rail fence using sawn rails was not common in earlier times but these days is the fence of choice for many horse establishments, especially those with valuable bloodstock. Commonly made with round treated pine posts and sawn hardwood rails bolted to the posts, they are usually painted either white or black. Their important advantage over wire fences is that they are highly visible, to prevent horses accidentally running through them, and there are no wires for the horses to catch their hooves and injure their legs.

The other form of post and rail fence using sawn rails was not common in earlier times but these days is the fence of choice for many horse establishments, especially those with valuable bloodstock.

A variation on the post and rail fence is the look-alike polymer 'strap' fence. Popular for horse paddocks, the 'rails' are made of a 10–12 centimetre strap of polymer welded to two or three plain wires which can be strained over long distances in the same way as a conventional wire fence. The straps are attached to the fence posts through brackets that allow the fence to stretch over its full length if hit by a horse, so avoiding injury to the horse.

As a further refinement the polymer can be impregnated with conductive material and connected to an energiser to become an electric rail fence.

Flexible polymer strap fences have become popular for horse paddocks. They provide good visibility, minimise injury and are easily constructed.

STONE FENCES

The limestone fences at the Kappawanta Station shearing shed on the Eyre Peninsula are among the most impressive dry stone structures in Australia. The yards and shearing shed are still in use.

Dry stone fences first appeared in Australia in the 1830s and until the 1850s they were rare in the broadacre farming areas. Fences that did exist were usually around homesteads to keep stock animals out of gardens and orchards or were built as stockyards and sheepfolds. When fencing became more common from about that time, stone fences were an economical choice in the areas where stone was plentiful and especially where suitable timber was not available and digging holes for posts was difficult. Where stone was available on site, the cost of building a stone wall was cheaper than post and rail and much cheaper than wire at that time.

Various styles and standards of dry stone fences can be seen on Sedan Hill, SA. BOTTOM PHOTO COURTESY OF SUE BRADSHAW

Stone walls in Australia can be found in Tasmania, on the basalt plains of Victoria near Camperdown, in New South Wales (notably around the hills of Kiama and Nowra) and in South Australia (especially from Strathalbyn to Jamestown and the Eyre Peninsula). Stone fences enhance any landscape and some of the most impressive are those found on Pine Hut Road near Eden Valley in South Australia, still in excellent condition.

Perhaps the most impressive stone sheep yards are the extensive limestone yards at the Kappawanta Station shearing shed on the Eyre Peninsula.

Stone fences generally served two purposes: one to contain stock, the other to use the stone that came from clearing the stony paddocks. It is difficult to know which was the primary motivation. Building a stone fence that would last was a job for skilled craftsmen known as 'wallers' who came from England, Scotland and Wales and from Germany and Switzerland.

Above, left: Limestone fences are common on the Eyre Peninsula in South Australia. This one incorporates wooden posts and a top wire to prevent stock from leaning over the wall and breaking it down.

Above: A mortared stone fence in the formal setting of the Kanyaka homestead. Kanyaka Station, 300 km north of Adelaide, was founded in 1852 and was once the home and workplace of seventy families.

Left: Limestone sheep yards on the Eyre Peninsula, SA.

Pine Hut Road near Eden Valley, SA, has some of the finest and most extensive examples of dry stone fences in Australia.

A team of one fencer, a labourer and two boys could be expected to build 20 metres a day when the stone was at hand.

Fencing styles varied according to the method of construction and the rock available, which might be sandstone, granite, basalt, slate, schist or limestone. Fences were either single or double skinned. The more robust double-skinned fences consisted of two 'skins' of 'fitted' stone that tapered towards the top, with the space between filled with rubble, usually with a layer of coping stones on top to join the two skins. The rubble interior not only served to clean up the paddocks but also provided stability to the fence.

The longest continuous stone fence can be found in South Australia, running for 65 kilometres along the Camels Hump Range.

It is estimated to have required 150,000 tonnes of stone to build.

Apart from their durability, stone fences were valuable as firebreaks. They were vulnerable to flooding, however, when water banked up against the fence until it finally gave way. While stone fences were ideal for containing sheep, considerable damage could be caused by horses and cattle rubbing against them and continual maintenance was required. Kangaroos 'flicking' off the top stones as they jumped over the fence were said to cause the most damage. Many stone fences incorporated wooden posts, allowing a wire to be added to protect the fence from stock animals leaning across it.

Stone fencing came into its own in the 1860s but by the 1890s could no longer compete with wire fencing and ceased to be a part of the rural landscape. Many of these fences are gradually crumbling away for want of maintenance and many others have been removed to create larger paddocks for modern machinery. But their importance to Australia's rural heritage is being recognised and more effort is being made to protect them, with several being heritage listed.

> The longest continuous stone fence can be found in South Australia, running for 65 kilometres along the Camels Hump Range. It is estimated to have required 150,000 tonnes of stone to build.

Part of the longest continuous stone fence in Australia, running for 65 km over the Camels Hump Range in South Australia.

WIRE FENCES

'Blind' fences, like this one at Allambi Station near Alice Springs, are made by hanging hessian over a wire fence to give cattle the illusion of a solid wall. They are commonly used in station country to funnel cattle in the direction required. PHOTO COURTESY OF IAN BRADSHAW

The availability of wire revolutionised rural fencing in Australia and had a dramatic influence on farm productivity and rural society.

Rolled wire became available in Britain in the 1840s and fences made of iron wire and posts, advertised as 'invisible wire fences', were promoted for their aesthetic value around parks and lawns. They were also 'guaranteed to resist deer, cattle, sheep and rabbits' though it is difficult to see how these plain wire fences would resist rabbits.

The first record of wire fencing in Australia was that built by John McHaffie at Phillip Island in 1842. An incredible 45 kilometres of five-wire fence was built using 00 gauge wire (9 millimetres in diameter). The cost of buying and shipping the 135 tonnes of wire required is not known but it must have been a very expensive fence.

Opposite and above: Pile driving steel posts at Flora Valley Station in the Kimberley and wiring up the fence to the welded steel strainer panels.

Above, right: The dying trees suggest this was probably dry land before the water table rose as land was cleared.

Right: This now redundant jam post fence once served to control rabbits, sheep, cattle and horses.

The fencing technique was to use a plough to create a mound with a ditch each side, and drive the posts into the mound every 5 metres with a 12 kilogram hammer. The ditch increased the effective height of the fence.

Tentative trials of wire fencing occurred in the 1850s, commonly using heavy 4 gauge wire (6 millimetres diameter – most wire used in modern fences is 2.5–3.5 millimetres diameter). This early wire with its various impurities was of poor quality; it stretched in summer, and with the pressure from stock animals rubbing and leaning against the wires. Many early wire fences were hybrids, with a single wooden rail on top and several wires below. As the quality of wire improved, thinner wire with increased spacing of posts reduced the cost of fencing. Increased post spacing required the introduction of droppers and wire braces to maintain wire spacing to prevent stock from pushing through the fence.

Opposite: The remains of a sheep fence, rusted by years of exposure to coastal winds.

Above: Concrete posts and steel star pickets are common in areas where trees are sparse.

Above, right: 90 mm netting fence was commonly used for sheep fencing before ringlock fencing became available. Attaching the wire with staples rather than drilling the posts has the advantage that a post can be easily replaced should it be burnt.

Right: Ringlock fence near the Stirling Ranges, WA.

Above, left: Hundreds of thousands of kilometres of wire fence with split posts has been built throughout Australia since the 1840s.

Above: Galvanised star pickets and ringlock has almost become the standard for new fences in sheep country.

Left: Cypress was the obvious choice for posts in the Flinders Ranges, SA.

Opposite: An abandoned fence of mulga and star pickets near Wiluna, WA.

Above, left: It is difficult to imagine worse conditions for fence building than those on Nappa Merrie Station near Innamincka, SA.

Above: The sloped fence at Manjimup Airport is designed to discourage kangaroos from crossing the airstrip.

Left: One of the farms fenced and ringbarked at Northcliffe, WA, under the Group Settlement Scheme of the 1920s. Some were abandoned and reverted to forest, others have become highly productive farms.

The posts of early wire fences were mostly augered to take the wire because the staples available at the time were too soft to use on hardwood posts. As the quality of steel improved, staples became an option for supporting the wire. The 1860s saw great debate in rural journals on the merits of various fence configurations.

Wire fence construction escalated dramatically from the 1880s, in part stimulated by the availability of barbed wire which had been invented in the United States in 1867. Barbed wire has since become a component of most modern fencing in Australia.

> Wire fence construction escalated dramatically from the 1880s, in part stimulated by the availability of barbed wire which had been invented in the United States in 1867.

An early version of high tensile wire available from 1897 provided for a more tightly strained, more stock-proof fence with fewer posts.

Rabbit netting was probably first used by Thomas Austin near Geelong in 1868. As the rabbit plague escalated, demand increased sufficiently by 1884 for John Lysaght to establish a netting factory in Sydney using imported wire. Prefabricated fencing (commonly known as ringlock or hinged joint) was available from the 1890s. In 1919 fencing wire was in such demand that BHP began making Australian fencing wire at Newcastle, bringing to an end the dependence on imports. By that time 2 million kilometres of wire fencing had been built in eastern Australia.

Further innovations followed, including the development of modern high tensile wire in the 1970s, which allowed for even wider spacing between posts and strainers.

Left, top and bottom: Kangaroos often find it easier to go under rather than over a fence. This 1.8 m ringlock fence with a high tensile plain wire and a barbed wire at ground level has been necessary to keep them out of this dairy farm at Yelverton, WA.

Above: Thousands of kilometres of fences have been built with jam posts in the wheatbelt and semi-arid areas of Western Australia. These small and often misshapen posts were readily available and extremely durable.

Opposite, top: A repurposed railway sleeper in a fence in South Australia.

Opposite, bottom: This much-repaired fence has now become redundant with a change to cropping.

Posts for wire fencing come from a wide range of sources, including split hardwood, treated pine, hardwood rounds of species such as jam and mulga, concrete, steel railway sleepers and even slate. But it was the Y-shaped star picket that revolutionised wire fencing when it became available in 1926. These steel posts, sometimes used alone but often interspersed with wooden posts, are easy to transport, easy to drive into the ground and produce a sound practical fence, especially when used with high tensile wire. Initially very expensive, they are now a component of most modern fences. Plastic sleeves that fit over the pickets are now available where insulation for electric fencing is required.

The emphasis has shifted from building a strong, solid fence that relies on the strength of the posts to a lighter fence with fewer posts that relies more on the elasticity of the wire.

ELECTRIC FENCES

The first electric fences were not used for stock control but to control people, using lethal levels of electricity. The Russian army used electricity as part of its fortification during the siege of Port Arthur in 1905 and the German army built the notorious Wire of Death along the Belgium–Netherlands border in World War I.

Electric fencing was developed for stock control in the 1930s in the United States but did not come into common use in Australia until the 1950s. The voltage used in these fences varies from 2000 to 10,000 volts depending on the length of the fence and the stock to be controlled – 2000 volts per millimetre of hide is required to have a deterrent effect.

A modern ringlock fence with an electrified top wire used to protect a heritage-listed split rail fence.

Despite the high voltage, stock fences are safe because they use very low amperage (about 120 milliamps) and the current is pulsed rather than continuous. Power supply can come from mains, battery or solar power. Even four D size batteries are capable of powering a kilometre of fence.

Standalone electric fences use insulated or non-conductive posts. The wood from some species of tree such as ironbark or mallet is so dense that it can be used without insulation.

Electric fencing is a cost-effective and convenient means of managing intensive strip grazing, whereby stock are moved every few days using temporary electric fences. Electric fencing is often used to supplement standard fences by running the wire through offset insulators to stop stock from pushing against them. These composite fences are frequently used for feral animal control.

Electric fencing is often used to supplement standard fences by running the wire through offset insulators to stop stock from pushing against them.

Although cheap and effective, electric fences have some disadvantages. One short can render the whole fence ineffective; vegetation can short out the fence if it is not kept clear; some animals learn to judge when the fence is off by recognising the absence of the ticking sound with each pulse of electricity; and some learn to 'grin and bear it' and dive quickly though the fence.

Insulated 'outriggers' are a common means of electrifying any type of fence.

FENCING FOR WATER

A dominant feature of the Western Australian wheatbelt and goldfields is the presence of large, bare granite rock outcrops scattered across the landscape. Their potential as a source of water was first exploited by explorer/surveyor Charles Hunt when he established a series of twenty-six wells from York to Hampton Plains east of Kalgoorlie in the 1860s. Many of the wells were dug at the base of these outcrops where run-off from the rocks had collected. These wells became a critical lifeline for thousands of gold prospectors and miners during the great gold rushes of the 1890s, and established the general route for the goldfields telegraph, railway and water pipeline that followed the gold seekers.

At Beringbooding Rock, sources of potential leakage are excluded by rock fences to maximise the water yield from rock catchments.

Much larger volumes of good quality water were needed along the railway line for the steam locomotives as well as the communities that sprang up along the way.

With no rivers and groundwater that was too saline to use, the solution was to harness the run-off from these rock outcrops. To do that, rock walls or fences were built around the outcrops to direct the water into channels and then into dams. Acquiring the stone for the walls was a laborious business. Naturally occurring slabs of exfoliated rocks were collected from the surface of the rock with sleds pulled by horses wearing hessian 'boots' to stop them slipping. Where more slabs were needed, wood was dragged from the surrounding areas onto the rock and set on fire. When the rock was hot the fire was then doused with water which had been carted from nearby wells and soaks. The sudden change in temperature caused the rock to exfoliate, generally in slabs about 80–120 millimetres thick. These slabs were then roughly shaped and cemented into place to form a wall. More carefully trimmed rock was then used to form the channels that ran to the dam.

The rock fence on Beringbooding Rock was built by sustenance workers during the Depression in 1937. It channels water into a 10 megalitre tank, still being used for emergency water supply.

Above: This 220 m steel aqueduct takes water from the 55 ha Karalee Rock catchment to a 50 megalitre holding dam. The dam was built in 1897 to provide water for the steam trains operating between Perth and Kalgoorlie. Page 65: Magnificent craftsmanship in the rock channels taking water from the Boondi Rock catchment to the holding dam.

These catchments are highly efficient. Depending on their size, steepness and the amount of patchy vegetation, they will yield 60–90 per cent of rainfall. Most importantly the water is clean and mineral free, which was critical for use in steam boilers. More than a dozen catchments of this kind were built to supplement water supplies for the Perth–Kalgoorlie railway as well as for the private 'woodline' railway that was used to supply wood for the mines and desalinators. The last of these catchments was used until 1953 when diesel locos replaced steam.

> With no rivers and groundwater that was too saline to use, the solution was to harness the run-off from these rock outcrops.

Several of these catchments have some noteworthy features. The Karalee Rock catchment has a unique steel aqueduct to carry water from the rock to the dam; the stone-lined channels directing the water at Boondi Rock are outstanding examples of the craft; and the rock walls on Beringbooding Rock are particularly complex to catch every drop of water. The catchment on Cardunia Rocks, about 100 kilometres east of Kalgoorlie, used to supply water for the Trans-Australian Railway, has the unusual feature of a large high-level dam and a low-level holding tank, once roofed to reduce evaporation.

In the 1920s many more rock catchments were developed to supply water for wheatbelt farms and communities. The dams for these catchments were designed to fill in years of below average rainfall. The last of these was built in 1995 when two hundred such catchments were still in use. Many are integrated with the Water Corporation's reticulation scheme while others are used as emergency supplies for farmers.

FERAL FENCING

This exclusion fence at Nangeen Hill Nature Reserve in WA, with its floppy top, wire netting, two electric wires and a ground lap, is an effective barrier against foxes and cats, providing a safe haven for the threatened black-flanked rock-wallaby.

The creation of sanctuaries to protect endangered species has prompted the development and testing of a variety of fences, particularly aimed at the exclusion of cats and foxes. These fences usually include a combination of netting fence at least 120 centimetres high, ground lap-netting to prevent digging under the fence and a fixed or floppy 'verandah' mesh at the top of the fence to prevent climbing. These may be supplemented with several electric wires alternating with earth wires to deter climbing. Thirty-millimetre mesh netting is required to exclude young rabbits. These fences are very expensive to build but are essential if the sanctuaries are to remain free of predators.

CATTLE AND SHEEP YARDS

A fine example of the use of available materials is the old sheep yards near Ardath in the wheatbelt of Western Australia. The yards are made from the metal boxes used to carry the 3.7 inch shells for the Vickers QF 3.7 anti-aircraft gun and became available with the closure of the No. 9 Advanced Ammunition Depot at Ardath at the end of World War II.

Cattle and sheep yards are perhaps the most interesting fences to study with their eclectic range of materials and methods of construction. This particularly applies to early outback yards where anything to hand could be incorporated. Apart from whatever native wood was available, farmers made use of railway sleepers, iron pipe, weldmesh, corrugated iron, stones, brush, wire, mallee roots, pressed metal and even ammunition boxes.

Modern sheep and cattle yards are sophisticated affairs. Frequently fabricated off site, they are built with a heavy emphasis on efficiency and the safety of both animals and stockmen and women. Designed to exploit the natural behaviour of the animals and the way they move, they reduce stress on the animals and the handlers.

Above, left: Old railway sleepers from the Trans-Australian Railway are a ready source of material for these sheep yards on Jaurdi Station, WA.

Above: Old cattle yards on the Talawana track are now just part of the landscape.

Left: Cypress pine, steel pipe and sheetmetal are used to make these sheep yards in the Flinders Ranges, SA.

Opposite, top: Disused cattle yards and loading ramp on the Dowling Track, Queensland.

Opposite, bottom: These types of wire strainer are particularly useful for short lengths and for older wire that is prone to stretching.

Opposite: These remarkable sheep yards near Bencubbin, WA, were built by the Pergandes family in the 1920s using rock exfoliated from a nearby rock outcrop.

Above: The skill of the builder is still to be seen at the cattle yards at Old Laura Station, Queensland.

Above, right: The race at the Kinchega shearing shed on the Darling River near Menindee made from the materials at hand – wood, bore casing, pipe, wire and weldmesh.

Right: One-way 'spear point' gate used to trap goats on the Darling River.

Top: Dog flaps in these undercover sheep yards reduce the workload of the dogs because they do not need to constantly jump fences to go from yard to yard.

Above and right: Many modern yards are often prefabricated by specialist yard builders. The curves in these cattle yards are designed to take advantage of the natural instinct of cattle to want to go back to where they came from. PHOTOS COURTESY OF COMMANDER AG-QUIP

THE RABBIT PROOF FENCE

The introduction of a few rabbits could do little harm and might provide a touch of home, in addition to a spot of hunting.

There can be few worse predictions than that attributed to Thomas Austin when he released twenty-four rabbits at his property near Geelong in 1859. Although this is usually cited as the origin of the rabbit plague that by 1900 was estimated to have reached ten billion rabbits, his were not the first to be introduced to Australia.

The First Fleet brought five rabbits to Sydney in 1788, to be followed by more in 1791. Rabbits were released in Tasmania in the early 1820s and by 1827 their numbers had exploded. Introduced into Adelaide in 1840, they were becoming a nuisance by 1864. Fortunately for Western Australia, of the five rabbits destined for the Swan River Colony in 1829, only one survived the journey.

An early example of a vermin-proof fence aimed at excluding rabbits and protecting sheep from dingoes on a Southern Cross farm.

Rabbits were probably first introduced as a food source, though likely not intended for the convicts, some of whom had been transported for poaching them. The later introductions by Austin and probably others were primarily for hunting by the landed 'sporting gentlemen'. In the words of one such gentleman,

> *We are so destitute of the means of enjoying country life as to have no deer, pheasants, quail, partridges and other creatures which afford so much enjoyment to gentlemen elsewhere. There is nothing here in the way of game for people of sporting proclivities and I have always found these gentlemen to be a most desirable element in a community.*

The 'success' of Austin's introduction is believed to be because they were a hardier breed of wild British rabbits than the domestic rabbit of earlier introductions. Their rapid natural spread was aided by deliberate translocation even after they were known to be a problem. While the Manifold brothers at Pomborneit in western Victoria (100 kilometres west of Geelong) were building a stone fence in the 1860s to keep rabbits out of their property, others were releasing them in New England, in the Barossa Valley and on the Murray and Darling rivers at Wentworth in New South Wales. In 1850 a man in Colac, Victoria, was fined £10 for shooting a rabbit on a property, but just eighteen years later the owner of the property was employing one hundred men and paying £5000 a year to control them.

By 1872 landowners had gone from urging the protection of rabbits to demanding their compulsory removal. Farmers used trapping, poison, fumigation and ripping of warrens, and paling and netting fences in an attempt to keep them out of their farms. Cats, ferrets, mongooses and dogs, from terriers to greyhounds, were used to hunt them and in the 1880s several shipments of stray dogs were rounded up and sent to country South Australia to assist in the rabbit hunt.

Above: Rabbit netting is used to protect this grave in the Flinders Ranges – ironically the grave of a rabbit trapper.

Above, right: An abandoned rabbit-proof fence in the Flinders Ranges. Successful rabbit control over the last two or three decades has seen widespread regeneration of cypress pine throughout the Flinders Ranges.

Right: This creek crossing in the Flinders Ranges illustrates the difficulty of maintaining the integrity of rabbit-proof fencing.

Ironically, station owners were at the same time demanding action to control domestic dogs that were attacking their sheep.

Rather than a barrier, the stone fence at Pomborneit became a haven for rabbits whose burrows beneath the fence were safe from ripping. More successful were the thousands of kilometres of wire netting fences built by individual farmers. The typical fence consisted of 1 metre of netting (17 gauge with 30 millimetre aperture) attached to the bottom of existing fences, with a minimum of 15 centimetres dipped in a mixture of tar and kerosene and buried in the ground. In 1887 the South Australian and Victorian governments collaborated in building 460 kilometres of rabbit-proof fencing, and in 1896 the Queensland government started building a 650 kilometre rabbit-proof fence near the New South Wales border.

At this distance in time it is difficult to appreciate the devastation of the rabbit plague. In 1900 the cost to agriculture was estimated to be £100 million, without taking into account the impact of soil erosion. Damage to pasture and crops drove many farmers off the land and banks were reluctant to lend money to farmers in areas infested with rabbits. There was another side to the economic impact of the rabbit plague, however.

The plague was also responsible for creating a major new industry. In the 1900s trappers were earning as much as a city tradesman and three times more than a farm labourer, resulting in labour shortages in many industries. Earnings from trapping were largely unaffected by

In the 1900s trappers were earning as much as a city tradesman and three times more than a farm labourer, resulting in labour shortages in many industries.

drought, depression or war. Rabbiting created a significant shift in wealth to ordinary workers and was the lifeblood of many rural communities – not to mention the thousands of boys who earned their pocket money by trapping and selling rabbits. Rabbits were sold for their skins and their meat. Factories were established in several rural areas to preserve and can rabbit meat.

In 1929 the rabbit industry was reported to be the largest employer in Australia. At that time in the rural areas and cities of eastern Australia, there were 20,000 to 30,000 trappers and thousands more working in transporting, skinning, preserving and retailing.

Between 1904 and 1947, 4 billion skins were exported and 1 billion were used locally, the price reaching 'a pound a pound' in 1946 – six years before wool reached the same level. In the same period, half a billion frozen carcasses were exported. Rabbits were also an important source of meat for local consumption and in the mid-1890s the Melbourne and Sydney markets were consuming 18 million rabbits each year, a rate that increased even further during World War II. The rabbit industry was estimated to be worth £3 million per year but the damage caused was estimated at £30 million per year.

For a time Western Australia was spared the rabbit plague but the Nullarbor Plain did not remain a barrier to them for long. By 1894 they had crossed the border. Surveyor Arthur Mason, sent to investigate the progress of the rabbits, recommended that a fence be built on the Western Australian border and another parallel fence 350 kilometres to the west (near Caiguna) to fence in the rabbits. A trap fence at the southern end would funnel the rabbits into the sea. Several hundred 'trained' cats were then to be released inside this area to eat the rabbits. It is not clear what would be involved in training the cats.

By 1898 rabbits had reached Israelite Bay, 500 kilometres west of the Western Australian–South Australian border, but were reported

Above, left: The No. 1 Rabbit Proof Fence near its start at Starvation Bay, WA.

Above, right: Additional wire and wire braces, as well as a lap wire, were added to the southern 300 km of the Rabbit Proof Fence in 1912 to make it dingo proof.

Opposite: The concrete wall that forms the start point of the No. 1 Rabbit Proof Fence at Starvation Bay on the Southern Ocean.

to have been virtually stopped by a large and already established population of cats in the vicinity of Point Culver. In light of this, 150 cats were released at the border but, according to reports at the time, most either starved or were killed by dingoes. Cats were also released at a number of other places in the goldfields but the program was limited by a shortage of cats. In any event they did not halt the invasion.

Given the escalating threat, a Royal Commission was appointed in 1901. It recommended the construction of a fence to stop the rabbits reaching the agricultural areas and was highly critical of the lack of earlier action. Surveyor Alfred Canning was appointed to survey the line for a fence from Starvation Bay (125 kilometres west of Esperance) to Cape Keraudren near Port

Hedland, a distance of 1833 kilometres. A daunting task under any circumstances, conditions in the northern part of the survey were extremely harsh due to the heat, lack of water and camel poison plant (*Gyrostemon ramulosus*). On one occasion Canning, having lost his camel to poisoning, was forced to walk 320 kilometres (120 of it without water) to his base camp.

Construction of the fence began in 1902, the survey was completed a year later and the No. 1 Rabbit Proof Fence was finished in 1907 – becoming the longest continuous fence in the world.

Building the fence was an epic undertaking. Because of the remoteness, lack of water, transport difficulties, uncertainty of conditions and the presence of poison plants, contractors were reluctant to tender for the work and prices varied widely. There was more to it than just building a fence. The job called for a 6 metre clearing with stumps grubbed out and holes filled; posts to be cut from available trees or steel posts transported to the site; a single wire fence supporting 1 metre of 25 millimetre netting, the bottom treated with tar and kerosene and buried 150–300 millimetres in the ground; trap yards (for rabbits) every 8 kilometres; gates every 35 kilometres; and camps for boundary riders every 45 kilometres. Stock reserves were also created, including a 13,000 hectare reserve for horse and camel breeding and for growing food for boundary riders' animals. Wells were dug where needed.

Because of the remoteness, lack of water, transport difficulties, uncertainty of conditions and the presence of poison plants, contractors were reluctant to tender for the work.

Section 4, from the head of the railway 110 kilometres north of Wiluna to Cape Keraudren, was by far the most difficult. Wire and steel posts were carted up to 450 kilometres from the coast or the railhead to the fence. Each 70 tonne load of materials required 560 camels in forty teams, each trip taking up to two months. Working on the fence were 120 men, 400 camels, 150 horses, fifty donkeys and five bullock teams. To safeguard the camels the last 350 kilometres had to be cleared of all poison bush for 800 metres each side before work could commence. Because they could not graze, the camels had to be fed on compressed oaten fodder, which not only had to be carted in but also increased their water demand.

Before it was finished in 1907 rabbits had breached the No. 1 fence, and two more parallel fences were commenced to try to stop their ever-westward movement.

Before it was finished in 1907 rabbits had breached the No. 1 fence, and two more parallel fences were commenced to try to stop their ever-westward movement. The No. 2 fence (1165 kilometres from Point Ann on the south coast to meet the No. 1 fence near Meekatharra) was finished in 1905 and the No. 3 fence (258 kilometres from the No. 2 fence near Yalgoo to the coast near Kalbarri) was finished in 1907 – a total of 3256 kilometres of fence.

But the work had just begun. The integrity of the fence was under constant pressure from fire, flood, shifting sand dunes, emus, kangaroos, camels or from people damaging them or leaving gates open. Boundary riders were engaged to maintain the fence using bicycles, horse and camel drays or pack camels for transport.

Left: Rabbit-proof fences were essential in most farming areas of southern Australia until the 1960s when the myxoma virus began to have a major impact on rabbit populations.

Above: Firing the stubble. This eighty-year-old jam and rabbit netting fence still has many years of life in it. These thin jam posts were used to build thousands of kilometres of highly durable fences throughout the wheatbelt of Western Australia.

The bicycles were specially sprung, three-speed models. Boundary rider duties were to repair the fence, empty trap yards, rake and burn leaves away from the fence and cut scrub and trees that were regrowing on the clearing. Some sections were as much as 250 kilometres long and took a month each way to travel. Shorter sections of 45 kilometres were covered twice a week. Supply wagons serviced the camps every two months.

In 1912 a decision was made to add two barbed wires above the netting and a lap wire on the ground to make the southern 300 kilometres of the fence dingo proof. By 1930 it was said that there were more rabbits inside the fences than outside because those on the outside died from lack of water in these dry areas, prompting calls to abandon the fence.

The fence was also a barrier to emus, camels and goats. The drought of the 1930s saw a mass migration of emus to the west and in 1932, twenty thousand were said to have converged on the fence, giving rise to what became known as the Great Emu War. An army machine gun unit was deployed to cull the emus. The operation was not a success and, in the words of ornithologist Dominic Serventy,

> *The machine-gunners' dreams of point blank fire into serried masses of Emus were soon dissipated. The Emu command had evidently ordered guerrilla tactics, and its unwieldy army soon split up into innumerable small units that made use of the military equipment uneconomic. A crestfallen field force therefore withdrew from the combat area after about a month.*

Nevertheless, the bounty system resulted in the culling of 57,000 emus in 1934 alone. A major drought-induced migration of emus has occurred about every fifteen years since then, resulting in the deaths of thousands of emus, cut off by the fence. The conflict between animal welfare and damage to crops remains unresolved.

The introduction of the myxoma virus in the 1950s had a dramatic impact on rabbit numbers and the fence became redundant for rabbit control. The northern section had already been abandoned, mainly because of the difficulties in finding workers, but also because it was now understood that rabbits did not survive in this environment. There were complaints, however, that the existing fence was exacerbating the problem with emus, which were being funneled southwards into agricultural land. In the early 1950s a new Emu Fence was built joining the No. 1 and No. 2 Rabbit Proof fences south of Lake Moore. Maintenance of the old fences was discontinued over the next two decades and a new 1170 kilometre fence was built from Ravensthorpe to the Zuytdorp Cliffs north of Kalbarri, using small sections of the No. 1 and No. 2 Rabbit Proof fences and the Emu Fence. It is now known as the State Barrier Fence.

The introduction of the myxoma virus in the 1950s had a dramatic impact on rabbit numbers and the fence became redundant for rabbit control.

Did the Rabbit Proof Fence make a difference? Certainly the fence did not stop the rabbits but it did reduce their impact and their rate of spread. From Geelong to the No. 1 fence the rabbits moved at the rate of 54 kilometres per year across some of the harshest country in Australia – but from the No. 1 fence to the south-west corner of Western Australia their rate was reduced to just 13 kilometres per year.

Is the State Barrier Fence any more successful in controlling emus and dingoes? Most of the Barrier Fence is currently built to emu standards but there are gaps in the fence and not all of it is dingo proof (which usually involves additional barbed wire and buried

Various iterations of the WA Rabbit Proof and Barrier fences. Later barrier fences are aimed at the control of emus and dingoes rather than rabbits.

or lap netting). Various proposals are being considered for its upgrade and extension to protect the farmland of the Esperance region. Dingoes are extremely resourceful when they want to go somewhere and the difficulties in containing them are perhaps best illustrated by the enclosures that are mandated in Victoria for captive dingoes. These must be 3 metres high with a 1 metre lap wire secured to the ground. The Barrier Fence in Western Australia and the Dingo Fence in the eastern states are not expected to prevent every incursion but to limit the numbers inside the fence and reduce their repopulation following poisoning or trapping, which is part of the overall control program.

Others argue that the fence causes the deaths of thousands of emus and kangaroos during their usual migrations, and excluding dingoes from native bushland inside the fence denies their ecological benefit in reducing the impact of goats, cats and foxes on native vegetation and animals.

Although most of the economic benefits of fencing for the agricultural areas adjacent to the fence relate to emus, followed by kangaroos, dingo control receives the most attention, partly because of the emotional impact of mauled and injured livestock. While the economic benefits and the threats vary considerably in different regions, there is strong pressure from agricultural and grazing interests to strengthen the Barrier Fence. The issue is controversial. Others argue that the fence causes the deaths of thousands of emus and kangaroos during their usual migrations, and excluding dingoes from native bushland inside the fence denies their ecological benefit in reducing the impact of goats, cats and foxes on native vegetation and animals.

No. 1 Rabbit Proof Fence
No. 2 Rabbit Proof Fence
No. 3 Rabbit Proof Fence
Barrier Fence
Proposed extension to Barrier Fence
Dingo Fence
Queensland Rabbit Fence

THE DINGO FENCE

The Dingo Fence is the collective name for several linked fences that contain the whole of south-east Australia, roughly separating cattle country from sheep country. Starting at the Great Australian Bight near Nundroo, the Dog Fence runs 2225 kilometres to the South Australian–New South Wales border near Broken Hill, where it then becomes the South Australian Border Fence for another 257 kilometres. At Cameron Corner it then runs 394 kilometres along the Queensland–New South Wales boundary as the Queensland Border Fence; it then leaves the border and runs 2500 kilometres through southern Queensland to near Chinchilla as the Great Barrier Fence. From there the Queensland Rabbit Fence (not part of the Dingo Fence) runs to Mount Gipps in the Lamington National Park. The Dingo Fence is administered and continually maintained by three states at a cost of $1 million per year.

The route of the Rabbit Proof and Dingo fences in Australia. The Dingo Fence has supplanted the No. 1 Rabbit Proof Fence as the longest continuous fence in the world.

Above, left and right: The dingo-proof fence has been built and rebuilt in a variety of configurations.

Left: The old dingo fence at Moolawatana Station, SA, which has since been replaced by a new electric fence (above).

Opposite, top: A double-width cattle grid is used where the Dingo Fence crosses the Eyre Highway at Yalata, SA.

Opposite, bottom: A gate on the main road through Hungerford at the dingo-proof NSW Border Fence on the NSW–Queensland border.

Page 97: Additional netting was added to this now redundant fence at Kilcowera Station, Queensland, to make it dingo proof.

At 5600 kilometres, it is the longest fence in the world.

Fences to control rabbits (in agricultural areas) and dingoes (in pastoral areas) were being built in all eastern states by the 1880s. Most of them were constructed around individual farms but there was growing support for the construction of more strategically placed fences to protect larger areas. By 1930 there were about 50,000 kilometres of rabbit fencing in Queensland, 70 per cent of which was private and 60 per cent had also been made dog proof by the addition of a top layer of netting. South Australia at that time had 75,000 kilometres of vermin fencing.

In the late 1940s agreement was reached to consolidate the fencing into a single continuous fence, running through three states. It took several years to realise and by then parts of it were in a poor condition. In the 1970s and 1980s much of the fence was upgraded and realigned to its present position. Most of the fence is 1.8 metres high but there are various styles of fencing. Some consist of netting with or without barbed wire, others incorporate 1.5 metres of lap wire laid on the ground, while other sections are plain wire with some of them electrified. Cattle grids are used at road crossings but at Hungerford there is a gate over the main road that crosses the Queensland–New South Wales border.

Breaches of the fence are inevitable. Apart from the threats of flood, rust and shifting sand, it is constantly being tested by emus, camels, wombats, brumbies, kangaroos and pigs. Baiting for dingoes along the fence and inside it are also a necessary part of control.

Maintenance is constant and in Queensland two-person crews patrol and maintain 300 kilometre sections on a weekly basis.

Maintenance is constant and in Queensland two-person crews patrol and maintain 300 kilometre sections on a weekly basis.

As with the Barrier Fence in Western Australia, there is considerable controversy surrounding the Dingo Fence. While pastoralists argue that raising sheep would be impossible without the fence, others argue that the absence of dingoes inside the fence has increased the population of kangaroos, goats and rabbits and therefore the competition for grazing. At the same time the controlling influence of dingoes on foxes and cats, by predation and intimidation, has been reduced, resulting in increased pressure on native mammals. Today there are demands to move the fence in the north-west of New South Wales to exclude the Sturt National Park in order to restore the balance in the park without adversely affecting sheep grazing.

VIRTUAL FENCES

There are an estimated 10 million kilometres of fencing in Australia today. But what is the future?

Trials are underway to develop virtual fencing for the management of livestock. Virtual fences involve animals wearing collars with sensors on them that emit a sound followed by an intolerable sound or a small electric shock when they approach the virtual fence. It usually takes only a few shocks before the animal responds to the sound alone. The position of the virtual fence is controlled by GPS signals and the fence can be readily moved using an internet or smartphone connection to the satellite. The 'fence' can even be programmed to move across the landscape at a steady or a variable rate. Proponents regard the system as more akin to a virtual shepherd than a virtual fence.

The cost-effectiveness of virtual fencing is still being evaluated but efficiencies in pasture management are seen as a major benefit in addition to savings in fence construction and maintenance. Whatever the future, there will still be a place for conventional fencing, at least for external boundaries.

Fencing our last claim on earth.

ACKNOWLEDGEMENTS

The information in this book draws heavily on the scholarship of several people as indicated in the list of books and articles overleaf. I am particularly indebted to the work of John Pickard and his endeavours to throw light on a previously neglected subject. I wish to thank Sue Bradshaw, Ian Bradshaw, Richard Shuard, Roger Underwood and David Jackson of Commander Ag-Quip who generously allowed me to use their photographs. I also wish to thank Margaret Wilke and Kelly Somers for their editing and for their helpful comments, and Ben Bradshaw for his assistance with the preparation of the map of the Rabbit and Dingo fences. I am particularly grateful to project editor Naama Grey-Smith, designer Tracey Gibbs and the entire team at Fremantle Press for their support and enthusiasm for the project.

The quotations in this book are from the following sources:

Page 28: *Western Mail*, 19 September 1903, p. 41, accessed online via Trove, National Library of Australia.

Page 45: Charles D Young and Company 1847 advertisement, reproduced in Pickard, J 2010, p. 29.

Page 77: Quote attributed to Austin, T 1859, cited in Kellet, M 2006, 'Rabbits in Australia: Who's the Bunny?' in *Australian Heritage*, Autumn 2006, pp. 74–78, accessed online.

Page 78: Cox, GH 1883, cited in Rolls, EC 1969, p. 23.

Page 88: Serventy, DL n.d., cited in 'Casuariiform', *Encyclopædia Britannica*, Encyclopædia Britannica, inc., accessed online.

Old tyres repurposed for rodeo and camp drafting yards at Carrieton, SA.

SOURCES

Photographs

The photographs are the work of the author unless otherwise accredited.

Newspapers

West Australian

Western Mail

South Australian Register

Sydney Morning Herald

Books and articles

Broomhall, FH 1991, *The Longest Fence in the World*, Hesperian Press, Perth.

Burke, S 2007, 'Fences, furrows, ditches and settlement policy: rapid landscape change in the Swan River Colony', *History Australia*, vol. 4, no. 1, pp. 03.1–03.15.

Crawford, JS 1968, 'History of the state vermin barrier fences', Agriculture Protection Board, Perth.

Dix, WC & Meagher, SJ 1976, 'Fish traps in the south-west of Western Australia', *Records of the Western Australian Museum*, vol. 4, no. 2, pp. 171–187.

Eather, W & Cottle, D 2015, 'The rabbit industry in South-East Australia, 1870–1970', in P Deery & J Kimber (eds), *Proceedings of the 14th Biennial Labour History Conference: Fighting Against War: Peace Activism in the Twentieth Century*, 11–13 February, University of Melbourne.

Fernie, B 1930, 'Water supplies from rock catchments in the Western Australian wheat belt', *Journal of the Institute of Engineers, Australia*, vol. 2, pp. 198–208.

Howard, B 2007, *Benefit-Cost Analysis of the State Barrier Fence*, Department of Agriculture and Food, Perth.

Laing, IAF & Hauck, EJ 1997. 'Water harvesting from granite outcrops in Western Australia', *Journal of the Royal Society*, vol. 80, pp. 181–184.

Leitch, B 2003, *Hearts of Oak: A Story Set in the Tasmanian Forests*, Southern Holdings, Rosny Park.

Long, K & Robley, A 2004, 'Part 2: Catalogue of fence designs', *Cost Effective Feral Animal Exclusion Fencing for Areas of High Conservation Value in Australia*, Department of the Environment and Heritage, Canberra.

Mosebya, KE & Read, JL 2006, 'The efficacy of feral cat, fox and rabbit exclusion fence designs for threatened species protection', *Biological Conservation*, vol. 127, no. 4, pp. 429–437.

Munday, B 2012, *Those Dry-stone Walls: Stories from South Australia's Stone Age*, Wakefield Press, Adelaide.

Pickard, J 2005, 'Post and rail fences: derivation, development, and demise of rural technology in colonial Australia', *Agricultural History*, vol. 79, no. 1, pp. 27–49.

—— 2007, 'The transition from shepherding to fencing in colonial Australia', *Rural History*, vol. 18, no. 2, pp. 143–162.

—— 2008, 'Shepherding in colonial Australia', *Rural History*, vol. 19, no. 1, pp. 55–80.

—— 2009, *Illustrated Glossary of Australian Rural Fence Terms*, Report HB 09/01, Heritage Branch, News South Wales Department of Planning, Sydney.

—— 2010, 'Wire fences in colonial Australia: technology transfer and adaptation, 1842–1900', *Rural History*, vol. 21, no. 1, pp. 27–58.

Rolls, EC 1969, *They All Ran Wild: The Animals and Plants that Plague Australia*, Angus & Robertson, Sydney.

Smith, K 1992, *The Settler's Guide*, Lothian Publishing Co., Melbourne.

Underwood, R 2004, 'The jam post and plain wire fence: an insight into York's agricultural, ecological and economic history', *Barladong: The York Society History and Heritage Journal*, no. 5, pp. 25–40.

Woodford, J 2003, *The Dog Fence: A Journey Across the Heart of Australia*, Text Publishing, Melbourne.

First published 2017 by
FREMANTLE PRESS
25 Quarry Street, Fremantle WA 6160
(PO Box 158, North Fremantle WA 6159)
www.fremantlepress.com.au

Copyright © Jack Bradshaw, 2017

The moral rights of the author have been asserted.

This book is copyright. Apart from any fair dealing for the purpose of private study, research, criticism or review, as permitted under the *Copyright Act*, no part may be reproduced by any process without written permission. Enquiries should be made to the publisher.

Printed by Everbest Printing Company, China.

National Library of Australia
Cataloguing-in-Publication entry

Creator: Bradshaw, Jack, 1941– author.
Title: Fences of Australia / Jack Bradshaw.
ISBN: 9781925164947 (hardback)
Notes: Includes bibliographical references.
Subjects: Fences—Australia—Design and construction.
Fences—Australia.

Fremantle Press is supported by the State Government through the Department of Culture and the Arts.

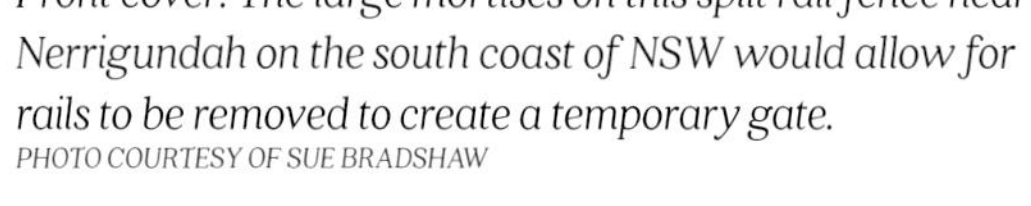
Front cover: The large mortises on this split rail fence near Nerrigundah on the south coast of NSW would allow for rails to be removed to create a temporary gate.
PHOTO COURTESY OF SUE BRADSHAW

Back cover: Paddy the kelpie on a visit to the stone sheep yards near Bencubbin, WA.

Endpapers: The yards at Allambi Station near Alice Springs need to withstand enormous pressure from milling cattle at mustering time. PHOTO COURTESY OF IAN BRADSHAW

Frontispiece: The ubiquitous Figure of Eight fencing knot.